Let's Talk About

THROWING TANTRUMS

Let's Talk About
THROWING TANTRUMS

By JOY BERRY

Illustrated by John Costanza
Edited by Orly Kelly
Designed by Jill Losson

GROLIER ENTERPRISES CORP.

Let's talk about THROWING TANTRUMS.

Some people show that they are angry by crying, yelling, hitting, and kicking things.

When people are showing their anger loudly and violently, they are THROWING A TANTRUM.

A TANTRUM is an outburst of bad temper or anger.

Whenever people do not do what you want them to do, you may become angry. You may want to throw a tantrum.

You may become angry and want to throw a tantrum whenever you must do something you do not want to do.

Whenever you cannot have something you want, you may become angry. You may want to throw a tantrum.

You may become angry and want to throw a tantrum whenever things do not happen the way you want them to happen.

Throwing a tantrum may cause you to hurt yourself or other people.

Throwing a tantrum may cause you to damage or destroy something.

When you throw a tantrum you may find that it bothers the people around you. They may decide that they do not want to be around you.

Thus, throwing a tantrum may be harmful.

When you are angry, you should never do
anything to hurt yourself or others.
You should also not do anything that would
damage or destroy things.

This does not mean that you should not
get angry. It does not mean that
you should keep your anger inside.

When you are angry, you may need to do something to get rid of your angry energy.

It's OK to cry, scream, yell, run, or jump up and down. It is also OK to hit or kick things that cannot be damaged (such as pillows, punching bags, or mattresses).

But *you must make sure that you do not bother anyone else while you are doing these things*. This means that you may need to go outside or into another room and close the door until you calm down.

After you calm down, talk with someone. Tell the person exactly how you feel and why you feel that way.

The best person to talk with is the person who has made you angry. If you can't talk with that person, talk with someone else.

While you are talking with someone about your anger, try to decide what you should do about it.

Think of what you could do to make things better.

Once you have decided what to do, do it.

Then try not to do things that will make you or other people angry.

Whenever you get angry, it is important not to throw tantrums that could harm you or others. It is also important not to do anything that might damage or destroy things.